GALE
CENGAGE Learning

Short Stories for Students, Volume 34

Project Editor: Sara Constantakis Rights Acquisition and Management: Margaret Chamberlain-Gaston Composition: Evi Abou-El-Seoud Manufacturing: Rhonda A. Dover Imaging: John Watkins

Product Design: Pamela A. E. Galbreath, Jennifer Wahi Content Conversion: Katrina Coach Product Manager: Meggin Condino © 2012 Gale, Cengage Learning

For product information and technology assistance, contact us at **Gale Customer Support, 1-800-877-4253.**

For permission to use material from this text or product, submit all requests online at **www.cengage.com/permissions**.

Further permissions questions can be emailed to **permissionrequest@cengage.com** While every effort has been made to ensure the reliability of the information presented in this publication, Gale, a part of Cengage Learning, does not guarantee the accuracy of the data contained herein. Gale accepts no payment for listing; and inclusion in the publication of any organization, agency, institution, publication, service, or individual does not imply endorsement of the editors or publisher. Errors brought to the attention of the publisher and verified to the satisfaction of the publisher will be corrected in future editions.

Gale
27500 Drake Rd.
Farmington Hills, MI, 48331-3535

ISBN-13: 978-1-4144-8583-6
ISBN-10: 1-4144-8583-2
ISSN 1092-7735

This title is also available as an e-book.
ISBN-13: 978-1-4144-8234-7

ISBN-10: 1-4144-8234-5
Contact your Gale, a part of Cengage Learning sales
representative for ordering information.

Printed in Mexico
1 2 3 4 5 6 7 15 14 13 12 11

The Widow and the Parrot: A True Story

Virginia Woolf 1982

Introduction

Best known for her experimental novels and short stories, Virginia Woolf also dabbled in children's fiction, although only one work, "The Widow and the Parrot: A True Story," is still in existence. "The Widow and the Parrot" is a fable-like tale concerned with an elderly woman, her kindness, and her eventual financial reward. The work is believed to have been written in the early 1920s. In the story, an aged widow, lame and impoverished, discovers that her miserly brother has died and left her a sizable inheritance. Attempting to collect the money, the widow, Mrs. Gage, makes the journey to her brother's home. She finds the estate dilapidated and ultimately worthless, but additionally learns that her brother had in his possession a parrot, whom she treats kindly. With the help of the parrot, Mrs. Gage eventually, after a series of trials, discovers the treasure buried beneath the floorboards in her brother's kitchen. Woolf's tale is often taken by critics to be an ironic interpretation of more conventional children's stories. While ostensibly a story intended to entertain and instruct children, "The Widow and the Parrot" is more commonly regarded as a satirical examination of the sentimentality and nostalgia of traditional Victorian fiction in this vein.

"The Widow and the Parrot" was not published in Woolf's lifetime. It was first printed in 1982 in the July edition of *Redbook* magazine. In 1985 the story was included in the compilation *The Complete Shorter Fiction of Virginia Woolf*, introduced and annotated by Susan Dick. A revised edition of this work was published in 1989.

Author Biography

Woolf was born Virginia Stephen in 1882 in London to Leslie Stephen and Julia Prinsep Duckworth Stephen. She was the third of four children. Educated at home along with her sister while her brothers were sent to school, Virginia benefited from her parents' literary interests and expertise. Her father was a philosopher, critic, and editor, and her mother wrote children's stories. She lost her mother in 1895. That same year, the young girl suffered her first mental breakdown. Over the next several years, concerns for her health drew doctor visits and periodic halts in her lessons.

In 1897, Woolf began attending classes at King's College, in London. She later studied at the Royal Academy Schools and took lessons from private tutors. Following a period of protracted illness, her father died in 1904. In the aftermath of his death, Virginia and her siblings traveled abroad, but in May 1904, she experienced another breakdown after returning to London. During this episode, she attempted to commit suicide. She recovered, however, and moved with her siblings from their former family home in the Hyde Park Gate district of London to a more inexpensive area, Bloomsbury.

By 1905 she was writing reviews and articles for the London *Times Literary Supplement*. She also spent time discussing literature and art with her brother Thoby's group of friends from Cambridge; the group came to be known as the Bloomsburys and included Woolf's sister, Vanessa, and her husband, a prominent art critic. The group also included critic and economist Leonard Woolf, who would later become Virginia's husband.

In 1906, her brother Thoby died of typhoid fever. She then moved in with her younger brother, Adrian, and focused on her writing. Following another breakdown, she was courted by Leonard Woolf and married him in 1912, taking his last name. Together the couple founded a literary press, Hogarth Press, and published works of experimental fiction by Woolf and others. In 1913, Woolf suffered another episode of mental illness after completing the manuscript for her first novel, *The Voyage Out*, which was published in 1915. She continued to write, publish, and relapse and recover for decades. Her works, including novels and short fiction, employ an innovative, experimental style in which she explores such themes as identity and sexuality. She additionally published essays and criticism and championed the notion of a woman's right to education, independence, and her own career, in works such as 1929's *A Room of One's Own*.

After completing the manuscript for what would be her last novel, *Between the Acts*, Woolf's health began to deteriorate once again. She drowned herself in the Ouse River on March 28, 1941, near the home she shared with her husband in Rodmell, Sussex, England. *Between the Acts* was published shortly after her death, but some of her works, including "The Widow and the Parrot," remained unpublished until years later.

Plot Summary

As "The Widow and the Parrot: A True Story" opens, the reader is introduced to aging widow Mrs. Gage, the protagonist of the story. Both lame and short-sighted, Mrs. Gage is also quite poor. She receives a letter from the solicitors Mr. Beetle and Mr. Stagg in which she is informed about the death of her brother, Joseph Brand, and the inheritance he has left her, including his house, stable, property, and a sum of money. Thinking about how miserly her estranged brother had been, Mrs. Gage is unable to muster much grief at his passing. Rather, she rejoices in the wealth she now possesses. After she borrows traveling money from her minister, Reverend Tallboys, Mrs. Gage makes arrangements to have her dog, Shag, looked after and proceeds to the town in which her brother had resided. She is offered a ride with a farmer, Mr. Stacey.

Upon arriving at her brother's home, Mrs. Gage is greeted by a woman from the village, Mrs. Ford, who directs Mrs. Gage's attention to the annoyances caused by the parrot Mrs. Gage's brother had owned. After Mrs. Ford departs, Mrs. Gage feeds the parrot a lump of sugar and promises the bird—James, as Joseph called it—that she will treat him well. Mrs. Gage then surveys the property, finding it to be in extreme disrepair. Mrs. Gage consoles herself with the thought of the money still to be claimed from her brother's solicitors, and she makes arrangements with Mr. Stacey to travel to

Lewes, where Joseph's bank is. The farmer warns Mrs. Gage about the dangers of attempting to cross the river at high tide. Arriving at the solicitors' office, Mrs. Gage learns that no money belonging to Joseph Brand can be found in the bank or on Mr. Brand's property. Dejected, Mrs. Gage begins the walk back to her brother's rundown home. Being lame, Mrs. Gage moves very slowly. By the time she makes it to the river, it is so dark she is unable to see the ford where the river can be safely crossed. She considers waiting until morning but is fearful she will die from the cold. As she deliberates "whether to sit or to swim, or merely to roll over in the grass, wet though it was, and sleep or freeze to death," Mrs. Gage sees a bright light illuminating the village of Rodmell, to which she is bound. Mrs. Gage soon realizes the blazing glow is a burning house. She makes her way toward her brother's house, and realizes that Joseph's home is the one burning. Nearing the house, Mrs. Gage fears for the safety of the parrot and asks bystanders if they have seen the bird. She intends to go into the burning home to seek out the parrot but is held back by the villagers, including the local minister, Reverend Hawkesford, and she is eventually led to Mrs. Ford's home to sleep for the night.

Unable to sleep, Mrs. Gage worries about the money she owes the reverend and how she will be unable to pay him, but is more distraught over the fate of her brother's parrot. She wishes she had had the opportunity to risk her life to save the bird. At this moment, she hears a tapping at the window. It is James, the parrot. He leads Mrs. Gage to the charred remains of his master's home, where he begins to pick at the floor in what was once the kitchen. Curious, Mrs. Gage investigates the area to which James is drawn and finds the bricks loose. She removes them and eventually finds the money her brother left to her, in exactly the amount stated in his will.

Mrs. Gage tells no one of her discovery and returns to her own home with her treasure and the parrot. Years later, the reader is informed, when Mrs. Gage is on her deathbed, she tells her preacher the entire story. She adds that it is her belief that James was responsible for the house being set ablaze and that through this act, he saved her from drowning in the river, and he then directed her to the money her brother had bequeathed to her. Mrs. Gage tells the preacher that she was rewarded for the kindness she has shown to animals like her dog and the parrot. James, the parrot, died moments after Mrs. Gage, several years after Mrs. Gage's dog had passed. The narrator concludes the story by mentioning that it is rumored that at the house's ruins, the parrot's tapping at the bricks can still be heard on certain moonlit nights, and some people have reported seeing an old woman kneeling on the floor in a white apron.

Characters

Mr. Benjamin Beetle

Mr. Beetle is one of the solicitors from which Mrs. Gage first receives a letter notifying her of her brother's death and of her inheritance. His partner, Mr. Stagg, informs Mrs. Gage that Mr. Beetle personally examined Mr. Brand's papers and property in search of the money he left Mrs. Gage. Mr. Beetle also reports on the "fine grey parrot," noting that his language is "very extreme."

Mr. Joseph Brand

Joseph Brand is Mrs. Gage's brother. As the story opens, she receives word that he has died. The reader is informed that Mr. Brand did not reply to the Christmas cards Mrs. Gage sent him every year and that his miserliness was a habit "well known to her from childhood." The state of his home indicates further either Mr. Brand's reluctance to spend money or his lack of wealth, for the property is dilapidated. Mr. Brand's miserly character is further illustrated by the fact that he has buried his money, stashing it away under the bricks in the kitchen.

Mrs. Ford

Mrs. Ford is a woman who lives in the same village (Rodmell) in which Mrs. Gage's brother Joseph had resided prior to his death. Mrs. Ford admits Mrs. Gage into Mr. Brand's home when she arrives. Mrs. Ford is irritated by the parrot, who had been shrieking "Not at home!" as Mrs. Gage knocked. Mrs. Ford explains that all day long the grey parrot sits on his perch and screeches the phrase. Mrs. Ford's presence in Mr. Brand's home is unexplained. Later, when Mrs. Gage is guided to safety by the light from the burning house, Mrs. Ford takes pity on Mrs. Gage, who, in Mrs. Ford's eyes, appears crazed in her desire to enter the burning home and find the parrot. Mrs. Ford escorts Mrs. Gage back to her own cottage, where she offers Mrs. Gage a room for the night.

Mrs. Gage

Mrs. Gage is the protagonist of the story. Poor, lame, and short-sighted, Mrs. Gage receives word that her brother has passed away and has left her with property and some money. She expresses not grief over his death but joy and relief at having been left with some means of supporting herself. In contrast to her lack of affection for her brother, Mrs. Gage lovingly attends to her dog, Shag, before her departure to claim her inheritance. She shows similar kindness to James, the parrot her brother had owned. Once she discovers that not only is the property that her brother left her virtually worthless but also there is no trace of the money he supposedly bequeathed to her, Mrs. Gage bitterly recalls her childhood with her brother. As she trudges through the darkness back to Joseph's home, she thinks about what a cruel boy he was, and how he tortured insects in front of her to torment her. She even supposes he is burning in hell at that very moment. Her despair intensifies when she realizes that she cannot cross the river in the dark without risking death from drowning, nor can she remain exposed to the cold all night without risk of freezing to death. Soon, however, she is led back by the light of a burning home, the very home her brother had just left to her. Her first thought is for the parrot, but she is prevented by the villagers from entering the home to save James. When James later appears at her window, Mrs. Gage demonstrates the great faith she has in James's intelligence by following him back to the burned home, where he guides Mrs. Gage to the money buried beneath the kitchen bricks. In secret, Mrs. Gage returns with the gold first to Mrs. Ford's cottage and then home, never telling anyone about the money, which she deposits in her own bank and upon which she lives comfortably with Shag and James for years.

Reverend James Hawkesford

Reverend Hawkesford is the clergyman in Rodmell, the village where Mr. Brand lived. As Mr. Brand's house burns, Reverend Hawkesford advises Mrs. Gage not to worry about the parrot, who he suspects "was mercifully suffocated on his perch."

James, the Parrot

James is the parrot owned by Joseph Brand until Mr. Brand's death. As the property of Mr. Brand, the parrot becomes part of Mrs. Gage's inheritance. Although Mrs. Gage's first introduction to the bird is made by an annoyed Mrs. Ford, who complains of the bird's constant screeching, Mrs. Gage finds the bird beautiful, though somewhat neglected looking. Mrs. Ford informs Mrs. Gage that the bird once belonged to a sailor and learned to speak a bit roughly. She also describes to Mrs. Gage how fond of the bird Mr. Brand had been and how he spoke to him "as if he were a rational being." Mrs. Gage feeds James some sugar, wondering if he is sad or hungry. She speaks gently to the parrot and tells him that she would make sure that "he was as happy as a bird could be." Returning home from her disappointing visit to the solicitors' office to find her brother's house burning, Mrs. Gage attempts to enter the home to find James, but she is prevented from doing so by several villagers. Once she has been safely brought to Mrs. Ford's cottage, Mrs. Gage finds James tapping at her bedroom window. The parrot leads Mrs. Gage back to the remnants of the home and begins pecking at bricks in what was once the kitchen, and in doing so, he helps Mrs. Gage find the money her brother stashed away. Later, Mrs. Gage not only credits James with revealing the treasure to her but also believes that James set the fire on purpose, in order to lead her home and guide her to the money, which she is certain could have been found in no other way. She later discovers that a kitchen stove had been built over the bricks concealing the treasure, and if the fire had not destroyed it, the treasure would never have been discovered. James dies moments after Mrs. Gage breathes her last breath.

Shag, the Dog

Shag is Mrs. Gage's dog. The reader is informed that Mrs. Gage is so devoted to him that she would rather go hungry herself than see her dog starve. Shag dies some years prior to the deaths of Mrs. Gage and James.

Mr. Stacey

Mr. Stacey is a farmer who offers to take Mrs. Gage to Rodmell with him. He likewise transports her to Lewes, the town in which the solicitors' office and bank are, and warns her about the dangers of crossing the river at high tide. On the way back to their own village, Mr. Stacey, who believes that Mrs. Gage lost all her property in the fire, offers to buy the parrot from Mrs. Gage. She staunchly refuses.

Mr. Stagg

Mr. Stagg, along with Mr. Beetle, is a solicitor who contacts Mrs. Gage regarding the death of her brother and her inheritance. Upon meeting Mrs. Gage, Mr. Stagg reports that no money could be found by his associate, Mr. Beetle, on the estate or in the bank. He furthermore advises Mrs. Gage to sell the parrot.

Reverend Samuel Tallboys

Reverend Tallboys is the village clergyman in Mrs. Gage's village of Spilsby in Yorkshire, England. He lends Mrs. Gage money to help pay her travel expenses to the neighboring town where her brother once lived.

Themes

Kindness

In "The Widow and the Parrot," Woolf explores the theme of kindness, specifically, kindness to animals. This theme is exemplified in the character of Mrs. Gage, who is unfailingly kind to her dog Shag and to the parrot James, whom she inherits from her brother Joseph. Mrs. Gage is described as "devoted to animals." Despite her poverty, she always provides Shag sustenance, even if she must go without in order to do so. Mrs. Gage readily befriends the parrot, treating him with sugar and vowing to take care of him. She is willing to risk her own life to save the parrot's when her brother's house burns down, and she ascribes to the parrot an enormous amount of intelligence, speaking to him "as though he were a human being." No other character in the story appears to share her love of animals. Mrs. Ford is intensely annoyed with the parrot. Mr. Stagg advises her to sell the bird. Reverend Hawkesford advises Mrs. Gage not to trouble herself over the fate of the bird, whom he believes probably suffocated in the fire. Additionally, Mrs. Gage is both pitied and regarded as a bit demented for wanting to save the bird.

The kindness exchanged between the human characters in the story is contrasted with Mrs. Gage's kindness toward animals. Although Mrs.

Gage treats the animals in the story with both love and respect, she exhibits little toward anyone else and is particularly uncharitable in remembering her deceased brother. However, Mrs. Gage is treated with kindness by many. She is obligingly carted from town to town by the farmer Mr. Stacey. The Reverend Tallboys lends her money. Mrs. Ford provides lodging. Despite the kindnesses shown to her, Mrs. Gage exhibits her own disdain for others in significant ways. First, she spares no kind thought to her deceased brother. She is initially joyful upon hearing of the inheritance his death brings, though she does feel grief. Later, she remembers his childish cruelty and his lifelong miserliness. Mrs. Gage goes so far as to reveal her vengeful nature: "I make no doubt he's all aflame this very moment in Hell fire," she thinks, "but what's the comfort of that to me?" When poised between the possibilities of drowning to death or freezing to death, Mrs. Gage rejoices when she sees a light that will be able to guide her home, thinking at first it might be a comet. Realizing that a house is burning, she thanks God, for it will burn long enough for her to find her way back. Disturbingly, she gives no thought to the people who could have been dying in the fire or losing all of their possessions. Arriving in the village to discover it is in fact the house she inherited from her brother, Mrs. Gage finds the villagers attempting unsuccessfully to douse the blaze with buckets of water. Her first thought is for James, the parrot, and in asking after him her kindness toward animals is underscored, shifting the reader's attention from the hardness in her heart toward humans back to her warmth and tenderness toward animals.

Topics for Further Study

- Woolf is better known for her adult fiction than for children's fiction. Select and read a short story from the 2002 collection edited by Woolf's husband, Leonard Woolf, *A Haunted House, and Other Short Stories*. Compare the story you chose with Woolf's "The Widow and the Parrot." In what ways, if any, are the stories similar? Are there resemblances in style, structure, or theme? Write an essay in which you discuss the plot, theme, style, structure, and characters of the piece you selected and then present your comparative analysis.

- Counted among Britain's modernist writers, Woolf achieved critical acclaim for her experimentation with the fictional narrative form. Like Woolf, French modernist writer Max Jacob also dabbled in stories for young readers. His modernist young-adult stories were collected in *The Story of King Kabul the First and Gawain the Kitchen Boy,* published by the University of Nebraska Press in 1994, fifty years after Jacob's death. With a small book group, read the short collection of stories by Jacob. Discuss Jacob's settings, imagery, and language. Thinking of modernism in terms of its departure from traditional storytelling methods, identify modernist elements in the works. What is unique or experimental about Jacob's language, style, and characters? How does he employ modernist techniques in ways specifically shaped toward the tastes and interests of young readers? Create a group blog where you and your classmates can discuss these issues. Describe your project and the initial responses of the group, and then allow individual members of the group to post blog entries where their dissenting opinions can be explored.

- Modernist poetry developed alongside modernist fiction, as poets likewise experimented with language, form, and technique. Kamau Brathwaite is an African Caribbean poet born in Ghana, a nation formed from the British colony of the Gold Coast. Using modernist poetic techniques, Brathwaite explores themes of race and identity. Study some of Brathwaite's poems, such as those found in his 2005 collection *Born to Slow Horses* or those in an earlier work from 1967, *Rights of Passage*, reprinted in the 1988 volume *The Arrivants: A New World Trilogy; Rights of Passage/Islands/Masks*. Select one or two poems and consider your responses to them, allowing them to inspire your own creativity. Create a work of visual art—a painting, sketch, photograph, or series of photos, for example—inspired by or related to Brathwaite's work. Alternatively, write your own poem, as inspired by Brathwaite's language, images, or style. Present your work to your class and discuss the artistic journey from Brathwaite's work to your own.

- Using print and online sources, research the history of the modernist movement in Great Britain. What political, social, and cultural events or movements helped shape British modernism? What writers were the first to be considered modernist? How were works by British modernists received by readers and by critics? Write a research paper in which you detail this history. Be sure to cite all of your sources.

Justice

Woolf treats the notion of justice in a way that reflects the conventions of the fable-like tale she has created. In this story, written with a young audience in mind, Mrs. Gage's kindness is rewarded and her brother's seemingly selfish intentions are thwarted. Justice is simple in the world of fables and children's stories, as children's notions of fairness are often quite stark: people should get what they deserve. In this story, they apparently do. Mrs. Gage struggles against her brother's efforts to "plague" her, even after his death. She suggests that he has led her on a chase after his fortune, believing that she would never find where he hid his money. After the parrot helps Mrs. Gage find Joseph's money, she feels vindicated, as "old Joseph's craft was defeated." In Mrs. Gage's mind, justice has been served. Her brother, she believes, is burning in Hell, and his plan to make a fool of her by leaving her money that could not be found has been foiled. In the world of absolutes in which the tale of "The Widow and the Parrot" operates, Mrs. Gage has been rewarded as she deserves, with her kindness toward animals repaid in material wealth, and her brother has been punished for his selfishness and cruelty as he deserves, with eternal damnation. The irony is that Mrs. Gage has not always been kind to humans, as her thoughts reveal, and the reader is left to contemplate whether or not justice has been served.

Style

Fable

Woolf's "The Widow and the Parrot" possesses a fable-like structure. Like many children's stories, it is structured around a moral lesson, and it further resembles a fable in its simple nature and in its clear depiction of hero and villain. The work features an omniscient, third-person narrator. In this type of work, a figure outside of the action tells the story and possesses a greater body of knowledge about the events than either the reader or the characters possess. In "The Widow and the Parrot," the narrator informs the reader of events that are about to happen, demonstrating her omniscient status, as when the reader is informed that "a great disappointment was in store for the poor old woman." Such statements additionally provide young readers with the sense that they are being told a story, even when they might be reading independently. To underscore the moral message in a fable or fable-like tale, writers often make stark distinctions between heroes, exemplifying goodness, and villains, who are examples of evil. Woolf does so by creating a sympathetic figure in the character of Mrs. Gage, who loves and is gentle toward animals and who is also poor and lame. Throughout the story, her willingness to sacrifice her own well-being for her dog or for the parrot is made clear. Through Mrs. Gage's recollections,

Woolf emphasizes the cruel, miserly, and calculating nature of Mrs. Gage's brother. His villainous character is described by Mrs. Gage as deserving of punishment in hell.

Irony

In the literary sense, irony is the expressing of meaning in language, terms, or conventions that convey the opposite of what that language typically signifies. The fact that Woolf is better known for her adult, experimental fiction than for children's fiction has led some critics to find irony in Woolf's usage of the typical conventions of fables and children's stories and to thus examine the story for evidence of deeper purposes. In fact, the story was written for the private, family publication Woolf's nephews had begun and was described by nephew Quentin Bell as "a tease." Bell, as quoted by Ann Martin in *Red Riding Hood and the Wolf in Bed: Modernism's Fairy Tales*, goes on to state, "We had hoped vaguely for something as funny, as subversive, and as frivolous as Virginia's conversation. Knowing this, she sent us an 'improving story' with a moral, based on the very worst Victorian examples." (Bell's statements originally appeared in the 1988 Hogarth Press edition of Woolf's story.) Despite the moral lesson demonstrated by Mrs. Gage's kindness to animals, Woolf weaves an ironic undercurrent, suggesting through Mrs. Gage's vengeful thoughts about her brother that she is not as kind as she seems and, in alluding to the brother's affection for the bird, intimating that his negative qualities may be overstated by Mrs. Gage.

The subversiveness Bell expected can be seen in the way Woolf employs some of the conventions of the fable genre in an ironic fashion. Many fables, for example, feature talking animals, and Woolf's use of a talking parrot in "The Widow and the Parrot" may be seen as an ironic take on fable conventions. She has not created a fantasy world in which animals, who often reflect elements of human nature, talk to each other but rather has incorporated into her realistic world an animal who can, in reality, speak. Seen through the loving eyes of Mrs. Gage, the parrot also exhibits "more meaning in its acts than we humans know." In this way, Woolf once again calls to mind the world of fables, in which animals possess the power of speech as well as the intellect of humans. By using the elements of the fable but doing so in an ironic fashion, Woolf offers what appears to be a tale with fable-like qualities, designed to teach children that kindness to animals is a quality worthy of emulation. At the same time, Woolf's treatment of her characters and the conventions of the fable invites adult readers to question her aims.

Another example of irony in the story can be found in Woolf's employment of a subtitle. The subtitle of the "The Widow and the Parrot: A True Story" suggests to young readers that events such as those that take place in the story can and have happened to people. At the same time, adult readers, and probably many young readers as well, in all likelihood are aware that the tale is a work of fiction. Moreover, some of the events narrated entail highly improbable situations. This serves as another example of the irony Woolf employs in various aspects of the work. In some ways, Bell's assessment was accurate: his aunt's story may be regarded as "a tease," one in which she teases her audience by apparently offering a children's morality tale but incorporating enough irony to encourage readers to analyze the story more closely.

Historical Context

Late Victorian and Edwardian England and Beyond

During Woolf's lifetime, Great Britain saw several rulers ascend the British throne. Queen Victoria ruled Great Britain from 1837 through 1901. Her reign is associated with an era of progress and prosperity, during which industrialization increased and the British Empire spread across the globe. The governance of India, a British colony, for example, was transferred from a private company to Great Britain in 1857, and Queen Victoria was named Empress of India in 1877. A strong supporter of imperial expansion, Queen Victoria remained an active and visible queen even during her later years at the end of the nineteenth century. She died in 1901, at which time the crown passed to her son, Edward VI. King Edward was fifty-nine years old when he took office. With an intense interest in foreign affairs, Edward served as king until his death in 1910. He was succeeded by his son George V, who held the office through World War I, which began in 1914 and ended in 1918. Although by this time the king had limited powers, George was a significant presence among Britain's soldiers. He visited troops and military hospitals throughout the war. In the face of German aggression in continental Europe, British popular support for the war effort was rallied through the government's emphasis on the rights of small nations to their own sovereignty. In the aftermath of the war, social-reform efforts for greater equality and a more democratic nation, which had been coalescing prior to the war, finally succeeded in bringing about changes in British policy. Universal male suffrage (the right to vote) was introduced in 1918, along with limited female suffrage, as women over thirty years of age were allowed to vote. Universal suffrage for all citizens over the age of twenty-one was granted in 1927.

British Modernist Fiction

At the turn of the century and during the first two decades of the twentieth century, writers and artists responded to their dramatically changing world—a world increasingly shaped by scientific advancements, industrialization, and warfare—by questioning the traditional modes of representation and expression. The developments in the world of visual arts, including the exploration of nonrepresentational forms of expression such as cubism (employing geometric shapes as the primary visual element) and surrealism (focusing on the visual interpretations of the unconscious mind), further influenced changes in the literary world. Paul Poplawski describes such dramatic shifts in perception and representation in his introduction to modernism in his 2003 *Encyclopedia of Literary Modernism*. Poplawski states that the "sense of living through a period of momentous social, political and cultural upheaval can be seen as a key motivating factor in the modernist insistence on an equivalently momentous upheaval in aesthetic practice." Writers such as Virginia Woolf, James Joyce, Gertrude Stein, and T. S. Eliot all explored a variety of narrative techniques, shaping innovative modes of expression and exploring stream-of-consciousness and nonlinear narrative structures. Particularly after World War I, a sense of alienation permeates works of modernist literature, as writers sought to perceive and respond to a world irreparably damaged by the suffering caused by massive worldwide warfare.

Compare & Contrast

- **1920s**: The modernist movement is transforming all forms of literature in Great Britain. Writers experiment with innovative forms of representation, exploring the psychological worlds of their characters; employing stream-of-consciousness narrative based on characters' inner thoughts; playing with words, language, and sound; and merging such genres as autobiography and fiction, or prose and poetry. The movement takes hold in America and Europe as well. Virginia Woolf, D. H. Lawrence, T. S. Eliot, Gertrude Stein, James

Joyce, Rainier Maria Rilke, Marcel Proust, and Franz Kafka are all writers associated with the modernist movement.

Today: Modern fiction has been influenced by the modernist movement in that modernism created new forms and modes of representation that allow many present-day writers to continue to explore innovative narrative techniques. Experimental fiction today often focuses on issues of identity and existence and questions concerning the nature of reality. Modern writers of experimental fiction include Shelley Jackson (*The Melancholy of Anatomy: Stories*, 2002), Mark Z. Danielewski (*Only Revolutions*, 2007), Ben Marcus (*Notable American Women: A Novel*, 2002), Liam Gillick (*All Books*, 2009), and Gabriel Josipovici (*Goldberg: Variations*, 2002).

- **1920s**: British culture is shaped by the recent events of World War I. In the aftermath of the war, the British enjoy the last years of the expansiveness of an empire, which soon begins to shrink as colonial territories seek independence. Social-reform movements lead to universal suffrage for British adults over the age of twenty-one. The prime minister during much of this decade is Stanley Baldwin. King George V, grandson of Queen Victoria, reigns over Great Britain during the 1920s.

Today: British society continues to be shaped by worldwide events, including the global economic crisis of 2008, which severely affected the British economy, and wars in Iraq, Afghanistan, and Libya, to which the British sent troops to support the efforts of the United States and the United Nations. Frustrated with the liberal Labour Party's handling of such events, the British people in 2011 elected a government dominated by the Conservative Party and led by David Cameron. Queen Elizabeth II, George V's granddaughter, has reigned since 1952.

- **1920s**: British fiction for children often combines lessons in proper moral behavior for children with discreet explorations of social issues, such as class conflict, poverty, or gender inequalities within families. Popular authors of children's fiction during this early period of the twentieth century include Frances Hodgson Burnett and Edith Nesbit.

Today: Modern British children's fiction is often created with structures similar to the works of Burnett and Nesbit in that social issues are sometimes incorporated into works ostensibly aimed at children. J. K. Rowling's "Harry Potter" series, for example, is infused with magic, mythical creatures, adventure, and explorations of identity but also contains elements of racial and social class conflicts. Angie Sage, in the "Septimus Heap" series, similarly creates a world of magic but one in which the young protagonists must find their true identities and places within a society troubled by discrimination and class tensions.

Children's Morality Fiction

British children's fiction during the late nineteenth and early twentieth centuries often focused on conveying a moral ideal or a set of social values to children. Although a moral lesson intended for young readers remained the dominant motif of such fiction, these tales also often incorporated commentary on current social conditions—commentary aimed at adult readers. Jack David Zipes, in the 1987 volume *Victorian Fairy Tales: The Revolt of the Fairies and Elves*, looks specifically at Victorian fairy tales, observing that writers of such stories "had two ideal audiences in mind when they composed their tales—young middle-class readers whose minds and morals they wanted to influence, and adult middle-class readers whose ideas they wanted to challenge and reform." Similar observations have been made about the more realistic children's fiction of the time period, in which the conventions of Victorian family life or social and class issues of the time period were criticized. Fred Inglis, in *Women Writers of Children's Literature*, edited by Harold Bloom and published in 1998, makes such a case for children's fiction written by Frances Hodgson Burnett and Edith Nesbit, both of whom center their stories around Victorian and Edwardian social values and morality but also address concerns about gender roles, the structure of the family, and class issues. Woolf's story likewise contains a moral theme aimed at young readers: be kind to animals. At the same time, she opens up for debate among adult readers larger issues, such as the established literary conventions she had a reputation for challenging.

Critical Overview

Woolf's short fiction historically has received far less critical attention than her novels. As Nena Skrbic observes in *Wild Outbursts of Freedom: Reading Virginia Woolf's Short Fiction*, Woolf's short stories, when reviewed, were often poorly received or disregarded by critics unable to interpret or categorize the works. In summarizing E. M. Forster's attempts to analyze the works, Skrbic finds that Forster characterized the works "as short, momentary post-impressionist portraits." Skrbic also analyzes the way Woolf's short stories "challenge generic classification by fusing a wide range of styles," as Woolf does with the fable and satire genres in "The Widow and the Parrot."

The humanlike qualities of the parrot, which link the story to the fable genre, are also commented on by other critics. Heather Levy, in *The Servants of Desire in Virginia Woolf's Fiction*, finds that the parrot is "forced to demonstrate extremely unlikely levels of insight in order to rescue [the widow] from her ineptness and greed." Other critics have focused on the modernism of Woolf's writing. Ann Martin, in *Red Riding Hood and the Wolf in Bed: Modernism's Fairy Tales*, claims that it is Woolf's modernism that informs her irony in "The Widow and the Parrot." She states that Woolf's tale "takes its ironic impetus from the Victorian sentimentality and pedantry that offended Woolf's modernist sensibilities."

This same sense of irony is noted by critics such as Wendy Martin. In her *New York Times* review of "The Widow and the Parrot," Martin claims that "Woolf's incisive irony undermines the conventional moralisms" in the story. She concludes that the work "does not capitulate to Victorian sentimentality as [Woolf's nephew] Quentin Bell originally thought it did. Instead, it is an amusing yet subversive story."

What Do I Read Next?

- Originally published in 1925, *Mrs. Dalloway* is considered one of Woolf's best, and bestknown, works. Tracing a day in the life of Mrs. Dalloway, its protagonist, the novel offers detailed and often psychological portraits of its characters. An annotated version of the novel was published in 2005.

- Woolf was a prolific essayist and wrote on a variety of subjects, including the art of writing, reading, women writers, and daily life in London, among other topics. The 2008 collection *Virginia Woolf: Selected Essays* provides an expansive sampling of Woolf's work in this format.

- Just as Woolf employed elements of fable and morality stories in her children's tale "The Widow and the Parrot," a number of recent young-adult novelists have been similarly inspired by the myths, folklore, and spiritual elements of various cultures and have utilized fable-like elements in their contemporary fiction. Chitra Banerjee Divakaruni is a native of India who writes such fiction. *The Conch Bearer* (2005) is the first book in a young-adult fiction series that weaves aspects of traditional Indian tales with a modern fantasy structure.

- Few, if any, modernist novels have been written with a young-adult target audience in mind, yet several coming-of-age novels by modernist writers, in their treatment of the journey from youth to adulthood, are appropriate for young adults similarly poised to make such a transition. Rainier Maria Rilke's modernist coming-of-age novel *The Notebooks of Malte Laurids Brigge* explores the life of a young Danish poet living in Paris. Rilke's work, originally published in German in 1910, is a distinctly modernist coming-of-age story that explores issues of identity and death. An English translation was published in 2010. The challenging work may be better suited toward older or more advanced students.

- Quentin Bell, Woolf's nephew, provides an intimate portrait of his aunt in *Virginia Woolf: A Biography* (1974).

- *Leonard and Virginia Woolf, the Hogarth Press, and the Networks of Modernism*, edited by Helen Southworth and published in 2011, offers essays by a number of scholars and provides a critical overview of the Woolfs' work in shaping the modernist movement via their Hogarth Press. The critics treat the themes of modernism as well as the social and political forces that influenced the movement. They also examine the works of some of the lesser-known modernist writers published by Hogarth Press.

Sources

Dick, Susan, "Virginia Woolf," in *Dictionary of Literary Biography*, Vol. 162, *British Short-Fiction Writers, 1915–1945*, edited by John H. Rogers, Gale Research, 1996, pp. 357–71.

Fraser, Rebecca, "Overview: Britain, 1918–1945," in *British History in Depth*, British Broadcasting Corporation Web site, http://www.bbc.co.uk/history/british/britain_wwtwo/ (accessed March 18, 2011).

"History of the Monarchy," in *Official Web site of the British Monarchy*, http://www.royal.gov.uk/HistoryoftheMonarchy/His (accessed March 17, 2011).

Inglis, Fred, "Frances Hodgson Burnett" and "Edith Nesbit," in *Women Writers of Children's Literature*, edited by Harold Bloom, Chelsea House, 1998, pp. 18–19, 99–101; originally published in *The Promise of Happiness: Value and Meaning in Children's Fiction*, Cambridge University Press, 1981, pp. 111–17.

Levy, Heather, "Halycon Spaces for Bliss: Heightened Class Consciousness, 1922–1926," in *The Servants of Desire in Virginia Woolf's Shorter Fiction*, Peter Lang, 2010, pp. 127–48.

Martin, Ann, "VirginiaWoolf: A Slipper of One's Own," in *Red Riding Hood and the Wolf in Bed: Modernism's Fairy Tales*, University of Toronto

Press, 2006, pp. 78–114.

Martin, Wendy, "Faithful James Fell Off His Perch," in *New York Times*, May 8, 1988, http://www.nytimes.com/books/00/12/17/specials/wi widow88.html?_r=1 (accessed March 17, 2011).

Poplawski, Paul, ed., Preface to *Encyclopedia of Literary Modernism*, Greenwood Press, 2003, pp. vii—x.

Skrbic, Nena, Introduction to *Wild Outbursts of Freedom: Reading Virginia Woolf's Short Fiction*, Praeger, 2004, pp. xi—xxiii.

"Stanley Baldwin," in *Number 10*, Official Web site of the Prime Minister's Office, http://www.number10.gov.uk/history-and-tour/prime-ministers-in-history/stanley-baldwin (accessed March 17, 2011).

Strachan, Hew, "Overview: Britain and World War One, 1901–1918," in *British History in Depth*, British Broadcasting Corporation Web site, http://www.bbc.co.uk/history/british/britain_wwone/ (accessed March 17, 2011).

"United Kingdom," in *Country Profiles*, British Broadcasting Corporation Web site, http://www.news.bbc.co.uk/2/hi/europe/country_pro (accessed March 17, 2011).

Woolf, Virginia, "The Widow and the Parrot: A True Story," in *The Complete Shorter Fiction of Virginia Woolf*, 2nd ed., edited by Susan Dick, Harcourt, 1989, pp. 162–69.

Zipes, Jack David, ed., Introduction to *Victorian*

Fairy Tales: The Revolt of the Fairies and Elves, Methuen, 1987, pp. xiii—xxix.

Further Reading

Bingham, Adrian, *Gender, Modernity, and the Popular Press in Inter-war Britain*, Oxford University Press, 2004.

> In this work Bingham analyzes the treatment of gender and social issues as presented in a number of British newspapers during the years between the two world wars, thereby offering a cultural and historical context within which the works of modernist writers such as Woolf may be understood.

Eliot, T. S., *The Waste Land, and Other Writings*, Modern Library, 2002.

> The long poem *The Waste Land* was originally published in 1922 and is collected here with a number of Eliot's other works. A contemporary of Woolf's, Eliot wrote modernist prose and poetry that similarly challenges traditional forms and structures and delves deeply into the inner worlds of the characters.

Ellmann, Maud, *The Nets of Modernism: Henry James, Virginia Woolf, James Joyce, and Sigmund Freud*, Cambridge University Press, 2010.

> Ellmann, a literary critic, explores

the relationship between psychoanalysis and modernist literature in this volume, using examples from the authors' works to offer a new perspective on the relationship between Freudian psychology and modernist writing.

Stein, Gertrude, *Tender Buttons*, Kessinger Publishing, 2010.

A contemporary of Woolf's, Stein published some of her modernist writings through Woolf's Hogarth Press. This volume of experimental poetry and prose presents Stein's reflections on the significance of everyday objects and offers a taste of her innovative experiments with language and poetic structure.

Woolf, Virginia, *Moments of Being*, Triad Books, 1978.

This series of autobiographical essays offers glimpses into Woolf's personal life, relationships, and opinions. The volumes are the only works of autobiography Woolf created for publication. Her husband eventually sold her diaries for publication years after her death.

Suggested Search Terms

Virginia Woolf AND modernism

Virginia Woolf AND children's fiction

Virginia Woolf AND short fiction

Virginia Woolf AND The Widow and the Parrot

Virginia Woolf AND Leonard Woolf

Virginia Woolf AND biography

Virginia Woolf AND mental illness

Virginia Woolf AND Bloomsbury Group

Virginia Woolf AND feminism

CPSIA information can be obtained
at www.ICGtesting.com
Printed in the USA
BVHW071047040822
643794BV00013B/631

9 781375 394390